Gazelle in the House

Lisa Williams

New Issues Poetry & Prose

A Green Rose Book

New Issues Poetry & Prose
The College of Arts and Sciences
Western Michigan University
Kalamazoo, Michigan 49008

First Edition, 2014.

ISBN: 978-1-936970-24-7 (paperbound)

Library of Congress Cataloging-in-Publication Data:
Williams, Lisa
Gazelle in the House/Lisa Williams
Library of Congress Control Number: 2013949845

Editor:	William Olsen
Managing Editor:	Kimberly Kolbe
Layout Editor:	McKenzie Lynn Tozan
Assistant Editor:	Traci Brimhall
Editorial Intern:	Dustin Brown
Art Direction:	Nicholas Kuder
Design:	Alexandra Levitin
Production:	Paul Sizer The Design Center, Frostic School of Art College of Fine Arts Western Michigan University
Printing:	McNaughton & Gunn, Inc.

This project is supported in part by an award from the National Endowment for the Arts.

Gazelle in the House

Lisa Williams

New Issues
WESTERN MICHIGAN UNIVERSITY

Also by Lisa Williams

Woman Reading to the Sea
The Hammered Dulcimer

Contents

I wanted, as it were, to see with my feet, connected to the earth.
—Charles Bergman

To an Exterminator

Because civilization is always
a retort to another's guts—

remove the hive. It is in
the wrong place, nestled and humming
as if error could become a home.
It needs your corrective violence.

For the hive attached to neglect,
built up in a lax, sodden Spring
in which no one was looking. Come topple
its walls, knock its symmetry's
struts. There are ways
to make disaster a part of our world.

(If the hive let us know it was coming.
If the hive had foreshadowed regret.
If the hive had not such dripping clamor

that destroyed what it met.) We need morning
swept free, as the drones clear the hive
of a hive's fine, antennaed
debris. Knock the posts
of its progress to dirt so we see what exists
now does not. Craft a lock
for the mind. Leave no sign
of vacancy.

Gazelle in the House

A gazelle in the house means tender, breaking
silence. An approach calibrating hesitation. Something
held out in the hand. Something bitter, exactly toward
a gazelle. You will bring things forward that are not
of your world. You will push things back that seemed
massive, fundamental—packed away, out of the path
of a gazelle. Rooms must be cleared for the strands
of her shadow, a thin frame on white walls. Let a gazelle
determine it all. Enclosure means trespass. What looks open
is. No thoughtless clarity. No space she cannot step
into, butt to the width of her animal
need. She will stray. Like a clock, her hooves mark
crooked shifts on your floor. Her ears
quake like tuned strings.

Thelonious

The tones like nothing done:
a thump, a slant lift, planks

of ivory opening, closing, sunk
behind: the rumble of a stone

caught in the clutter of a creekbed
under water's rush: the crooked

passage that a flood can settle:
nuanced tread, asymmetrical

ramble only he could muster
from the backward drift of fingers: chords

part Ellington, part the end
of melodious as we know it: weird

time striving, wayward mind
trilling to the ground.

Torch

. . . when I beheld a fire win out
against a hemisphere of shadows.
—*Inferno*, translator Allen Mandelbaum

If I could hold a fire against
a hemisphere of shadows, hold it
close, not so that damage
finds my hands, but so fire scatters
galvanizing strands, my pupils
responsive to the flames' unbridled
tutelage as they tell me
nothing but these little jumps
out of your definitions, small
or large or leaping, sinking, slumped . . .
If I could hold a fire against
that lattice-work of shadows, standing
close to flames pivoting without
being singed or riveted or convinced
it is the only spirit, like a god,
making me something nailed to wood
then keep my head, then coolly draw
some backbone from that dazzle.

Mistral

The wind is not your companion.
Nor is it whispering anything to you.
Nor is it not whispering.

It is not a transparent, invisible thread.
It is not a rhythm undenied.
It takes the pine tree on its way and takes it
to the outer reaches of tree
so all its needles bend shaking.

It can exact the opposite
of what things are known for
but only partly.

When it is over you can best imagine it—
Lying, just a cat in a cage.

It pushed the latches but not for truth.
Inside no different.
Math to its whim.

You couldn't phrase its body,
shape, when
it comes, out of a time, and encounters
and countering *and*.

Shoot

for Suzanne Opton

She wants to photograph singers singing,
mouths opened wide, hands splayed,

eyes in the liquid of a note,
throats curved, offering. But it's the gesture

that interests her, that body in
a space. The singing is the engine

of that gesture. Or the water. Or the fire
that fills the flesh, like a balloon,

with purpose, gives it pause,
how a body avails itself of space,

arms encountering air,
legs steadfast, chin tilted up.

The singer says: *To sing, the chin should be tucked.*
It's how we hold ourselves.

But the photographer wants the throat
swanned, that human span

of soft determination between brain and bone.
She asks the singer to lift his head while singing.

They argue gently. She may not win after all,
the singer knowing only that the picture

will be of him, singing. The photographer,
she wants that dialogue between a singer's gesture

and what slants it—her desire
for a certain frame in space,

matter's demands on circumstance, who knows.
Where the two meet, whether they do,

is neither hers nor the singer's
to predict. A pressure. An encounter.

Nucleolus

I can grow in shadow as in light.
I can grow in shadow, I promise you.

As in light. Only the dark minds those little
fingers. Only

the dark, considering, reveals.
As in light when the veining

trembles. As in light with its petalled
ends.

A thousand thousand shoulders inside shadow
bear weight.

Like soil the shadow,
shadow for hands. I can grow

in a pool of it. Unlike blaze
where figures sharpen. I handle

and I grow in it
I promise you. As with loss

deciphering to
myself and through. Through.

Composition of the Moon

No more movement. Hanging more distant.
First silver, then sliver, then knives.
Girl grown into silence, grown small, is that it?
Then drifted without notice away.

First silver, then sliver, then knives.
Once so close, glowing down, glowing up,
then drifted without notice away,
your mouth a saliva of questions.

Once so close, glowing down, glowing up
and brighter: you talked to it then,
your mouth a saliva of questions.
What is not there you know now. What not

and brighter, you talked to it, then
teeth bar the word beauty like prey.
What is not there you know now, what not
to see, after seeing has fallen,

teeth bar the word beauty like prey.
Girl grown into silence, grown small, is that it?
—to see, after seeing has fallen,
what's lost? After saying, not say?

Leaving the Field

The grove we approach looks dark as a wound
we'll enter, as the cicadas drone
through leaves with an off-key, faltering hum
that strengthens as it resolves. *You are down,*
it intones and we are: still, separate from
cicadas that vibrate on limb after limb
in slurred, ragged waves of excitement, flung
by the monumental furnace that drives them.
The wires and caverns of burning life seem
intensely their own, to those of us listening.
The fact is, they don't know we listen,
don't care, and don't say a thing that's human.
Their sound is a strong and useful change
to us, who believe we are used to change.

Irony

What have you done with my chiming?

I can't be alone here
and you must forge
sharp rapport with your longing,

must
snap quickly back—

it seems a way.

How dry the land
out of music,

pressed
to deny.

Varying Lines

Things are only themselves in this light.
So if Cezanne

painted the tree trunk in the foreground
of the mountain with a sliver

of the mountain in front of it
like the finger of a hand that grips

preventing the tree from falling
into our vision,

the reason is the mountain participates,
as does the tree, its bark,

and what appears to be an error
is faithfulness:

the mountain
inhabiting the mountain

past the brush stroke,
the tree placed forward held back.

*

As if to say
I seek a balance.

I seek a place to stand
from where I can also listen.

*

(The Bathers)

You could say all elements of this landscape
are one—but that could not be.

Yes, the air *trembles* with the colors of leaves.

The pool the bathers have stepped into is
a well of colors like all the rest.

What the eye sees as bodies is what the eye knows.

The men recognize this. They are kin in abandon.

One looks as if he is listening carefully
to all the particles announce themselves,

as if he might be absorbed, sublimely disintegrate,

his body arched slightly, arched the way
the tree limb arches, almost a hand dipping into the pool.

He is attending to the air, to something farther
than his companions. His back turned to the onlooker,

he listens.
Or does he shout?

*

(Figural)

Cezanne does not let him come beyond the paint.
That is its purpose—
to set a man there, thinking, before us,
the man's hands gripped as if they hold onto themselves.

That is its purpose
and nothing else—a body—
the man's hands gripped as if they hold onto themselves
composed of reds, browns, and golds

and nothing else—a body—
and inside one closed fist, blackness
composed of reds, browns, and golds
because that's what it is, flesh in a place

and inside one closed fist, blackness.
Even his hand resting on his thigh fights for its place
because that's what it is, flesh in a place
surly and impartial as the apples piled on the table beside.

Even his hand resting on his thigh fights for its place,
so much himself that we see him only,
surly and impartial as the apples piled on the table beside,
not ourselves, not him looking where we are.

If Language Is a House of Being . . .

The house grew around you
as you built it, then stayed.

You like one of its corners come up short.
You like that your foot does not stumble
where another's stumbles

and the window that looks out
to nowhere, stars spun unto black—

that was your view, yours
to point at, mouth gaping.

Such homespun, hammered
dynasty, pieces you found,
pieces you made,
arrangements that appear ridiculous
to the onlooker—

These were your joints
of settlement and turn.

Up to the visitor now
to enter,

stonecutter
you never were.

Villa Medusa

Fiddler Crab

To travel sideways—
lunging at the world with one

big claw, lopsided vision,
junk-heap of evolution's

elbows, prongs, and hinges,
uncommitted to the surface, skimming

warily—you bolt,
are poised even when still

to withdraw at the slightest
tremor, a shadow's digit,

your adventures thin compared
to the incremental journeys of a snail

(effusive as pleasure,
each blade of texture

wallowed and soiled),
with brittle fidgets touch

little to keep you here, scuttle
again and again

as if slung by a rubber band
or yo-yo'd

from the corkscrew
involution of your burrow

which you will back in,
blocking

claw held aloft, bulged
eyeballs on the intruder, withholding

your lightless, shallow, brief
interior.

Villa Medusa

It goes without saying that Haeckel reduced the organisms he beheld to the basic pattern of symmetry that interested him.
—introduction to Ernst Haeckel's
Art Forms in Nature

Down, the filigraic
radiolaria spines

combed from the briny womb
they whirled in, skeletons

like radiant spheres or suns.
Down, he drew them. Dry,

out of hiding, so that they were
magnifying westward

on his page, large,
out of scale. He was some god

of drawing. And others fell
for them too: as ornament,

motif; a chandelier;
the gate of a world's fair.

From single-celled, roseate
marvels built "like crystals"

he said, to anemones, bats,
octopuses, antelope crowns,

until the most admired
of his swollen resolutions,

that painted, toxic queen,
a fantastic jelly, reigned

as "ceiling decor": the Medusa
in his house, the Villa Medusa.

Octopus

In my room, I can conceive of your
splayed arms combing

water's bluish weight, your skin
vacillating as you shudder

from one long shadow at the seafloor
to another. I believe your head

is bulbous as a human infant,
that you have a surface temperament

tender as a heart's
and quick to judge, that you live

shrunken without touch, soft and indrawn
from rock walls, where you cogitate

in hollows till provoked,
stung out of your dreaming

to veils of seawater and silt.
You raise furious color wheels

like Ezekiel's cherubim
when afraid. Not so different

from the grasping mind.
Except that you are arms following mind.

Brooding Eels

They are circling   circling   wanting a way to the sea
the urge to spawn comes   the urge to spawn goes

there is no way to swim to the sea   they are
circling   growing bigger   growing tremendous

they lift heads now huge out of water to smell
air   whether there will be a change

so they can swim to the sea   (a rock
slide blocks their way from the lake

to the sea)   they are circling for decades
their skin thickens   their eyes cloud   they are ready

the urge to spawn comes   the urge to spawn goes
they will die some day   they will never

die   there is no way no way
to the sea   breeding is necessary   brooding

is what happens   will there be a chance a storm
or just this ache for distance another century?

Aquatic Herd

—rainy season, Lake Chad, Niger

A tangle of white horns
bristles above the line of water
you swim to graze, your pasture

those foliaged margins steeped in
accrual, like a word you can hear,
the hiss and rustle of bodies

plying wheels of water, the grind
of your teeth on familiar flourish.
Morning frays from the lake

this hour you don't
know barrenness, dry
stretch of sand without a trickle

or bloom. At home near algae,
near succulent moss, hooves scribbling
bottom layers,

helpless
to those who could see you graze,
you might look dangerous.

Bodies hidden. Just heads
crowned with ghostly architecture—
a stripped and estranging forest,

all branches. Or hollow spines.

Pelican Eye

The eye of the pelican
bares a plain surface,
black center, yellow rim
or "ring," depending on
how you say it—rim
leading to edge, ring
leading to marriage (a ledge
you circle or fall from, or a circle
of gold). If the eye
of the pelican had a voice,
it would speak plainly.
It wouldn't mince verbs
and it might lash out
like a frog's sticking tongue
or infold like a quartz,
prickly with elements.
The eye of the pelican
if it could listen
would hear discretely:
the blunt squeak and moan
of its young, its bone
-engined wings, the hinged
accordion note
of its fleshy throat sack
slipping with scooped,
silver fish—but I
have lost track. Or have I
been looking? The eye
of the pelican wingbeats
me back.

Mayhem

Take from me myself
all I know as mine
bound into a center,

explode it out
but delicately, to the tendrilled
end of each arm.

Seeing courses
to other veins
sight horizontaled, and I

am actual,
more than actual.
My body looses freight.

Borne out, I witness.
The giant octopus,
rippled gray for sleep,

scarlet for action,
her form a needle
then a splay,

soon knits
her plume of eggs
to a fibrous web

she'll gentle suction over
hourly, with such care,
and starve to tend, then

just before dying, lightly
blow them past
her arms.

Anemone

To first see you is to be numbed
by the fluid weaponry of your arms
lilting and falling in the tidepool's
sheer excitements.

You are the hue
of delicatest violet. Fierce persimmon.
Solipsistic blue.

Above the womblike, rippling chamber
of obvious tendrils, some new
visitor sails, your mouth hidden,
motive and its engines concealed.

Almost anything that touches you
is yours. How can you seem
foreign to us who so often
surround, draw forward, and then close
over, even as we gesture,
a separate body?

I know this need to encompass
and seize with delirium's lines.

Oceans

Lunge because of the vacuum
you live in and because the neglected
edges you touch with your rim
brood bodies you've protected,
twined vitals in the mass
of water dragged behind you.

Sharp or gelatinous,
so much I consider true
darts or spirals in your hived
enclosures. Long-held obsessions
swollen to repetitive
unfoldings, the heroine's
encounters with an obstacle,
imaginings spun to a fringe
outside of which her figures crawl?

—I simplify. Stay wavering
and many, a spectrum's harbor
more than "azure indolence,"
each drop for each occasion your
inviolable firmament.

Sounding Line

When you hove the plumb in the ocean
you heard it break the sheen
on the surface as it parted walls
of the mutable water column

then a rasp as your hands passed over
the visible twist of the rope
as the line paid out, and you wondered
how deep it would have to go

(your fathoming tool) as it sank
through layers of photosynthetic
migrating cells and stories
of diatomic bodies

until, once the lead hit the floor
with a slight change in slack, you could tell
how far the eye had travelled
by marks tied on the line

so that you pulled the weight
back up the glassy staircase,
back to the euphotic surface
where the ship steadied the plumb

and where, in a repetition
like a watery palindrome,
you—bound and leaning—were reeling
the measured feeling home.

"The Swallow That Hibernates Underwater"

—hypothesis of 19th century naturalist,
Gilbert White

He kept them close. He dreamed their weight in water,
brain a dome of swerves under the clouds,
the pond a quiet shell, iced-over drift,
wings slick, ethereal purpose dormant

—just what he thought the swallows' months
of cold meant: in pond shallows, tucked
where they could safely winter, breathing
brains a void of swerves under the clouds

that overarched such acrobatic dips
in spring and summer for ripe ephemerals
they'd catch. They'd clarify the air. Agile,
he kept them close. He dreamed their weight in water.

Bells Buried under the Sea

A slow and ghostly alteration.
A heaviness at the center and all sides.

There was no tower fallen in the ocean.
There was no tide that rose above the tide

and higher, to swallow a tower's town.
Instead the bells were strapped on a ship that sailed

to a tiny village, newly campaniled
but during a storm, the crew heaved the bells

overboard to lighten the ship's burden
and this had saved them all. A near

disaster was how "bells" diverged
from being what they were, from being heard,

beauty most moving when it's muted,
impossible to speak up. How the giant,

cast, important contours jangled down
brocaded bolts of the abyss

past slanted, steep embankments,
too deep for pretty names.

The Hummingbird Aviary

Blind Crevasse

—Polar explorer Richard Byrd

Hand by hand, over blistering slivers
of ice scraping wrists and slithering in ears,
hand by hand, with ferocious delicacy,
a furnace burning behind your efforts,
you pull your body away from that
crevasse, stand up, look back at what
you avoided, widening from one crack
to a vaster chasm hundreds of meters
down, sapphire, then emerald damask
on vertical plunging walls, an endless
corridor of spiked sea glass—

You were cheek on crystal, in a terrible fallen
field, your left leg dangling over
the roof of a crater toothed with punched
translucence. Ecstatic to leave the past,
to have glimpsed its Kublaian center, you
walk in an opposite direction

but it's still close to you sometimes,
half-lit, a story you might enter,
a submerged star, its azure pinnacles
ruminant. Did you think it wouldn't
fool you again, since you are safe
from its jewelled, devouring throat, the masked
abyssal draw of its depression
covered by a fresh and blinding snow?

Bees in a Time of War

It's not the bees but the shadows of the bees
arcing over the surface of a field.

Down, then over. Up, and then across,
their bodies skimming the weedy surface

like thoughts. Or like a mass of thoughtless shapes
moving, only moving, and not meaning,

the bees' quick bodies and the bodies' shades
bullet-shaped, but much too soft

to be bullets. Much too gentle, visibly
flitting over green pennants of grass.

Maybe a shadow is a body's penance,
its penalty for moving across a field,

across so many blazing surfaces
like this grass arcing out of amassed soil.

Or maybe some dichotomy has failed,
the bodies and the shadows of the bees

in their slightly shifting pattern making forms
that are random: ovals, circles, angling reels,

the shadows marking darker, lowering
wheels that both undermine and propel

the fact that the body of a bee exists,
that something shifts under its vibrant buzz

moving almost silently without cause,
building and building a field of bodies.

Desert Appearance

—after a phrase by Francis Bacon

"To be able in a portrait to make
a Sahara of the appearance." Make
a desert of the familiar or
an oasis of pooled distance. Like
a mirrory montage in which things
look alike but seem different, a *seeming*
aimed at blasting through the eye's
impediments. To witness. Showing
what it is as if it isn't filled
with what it's thought to be. A Sahara is
—for you, for me—far, foreign, and siroccoed,
golden with swarmed sand and buried moments. Make those
knowns gnash unfamiliarly. Combine
experience with randomness
of mind, of flesh. Let appearance appear to be
less than its particles—and more. A monument
of something malleable. Held, but wavering its grains.
Both disparate and ordered. Skilled, but scrambled in its means.

Transparent Journey

To travel across the glass mountain,
the princess must hold three silver needles
long as her arms to puncture the glass:

one shoved in to step on, two
shoved in above that to heave herself
up with: punch the glass, heave, step, pull, over

and over, without losing rhythm or heart.
The floating clouds are sacs of water
she is terrified will spill.

What is in her mind at these moments?
To travel across the glass mountain
for what is on the other side.

Don't look around. Don't look around. She tells herself
this not-song as she rallies her procession,
three needles growing hot in her hands.

The Hummingbird Aviary

Step into it: they radiate,
hover, reconnoiter, whirring past guests,
past the girl, mouth agape, in a yellow

t-shirt, the men with cameras and caps, the women
with cameras and sunglasses, all the cumbersome slack
of what we are and have become in an eternal

hummingbird paradise—quick—there's one
emerald-throated propeller-winged phantom
of a bird, not a bird, a spirit, a sprint,

like an arrow that missed us. See the miniscule nest
in the crook of a cluster of leaves, and the baby bird
struggling to move, drab and gasping, beak

cracked? The mother lights down to feed
the flute-hole of its throat—it's a smudge,
an inkling, this not-yet-grown

hummingbird—it would smear
if you touched it. The mother takes off. Pause
while you focus, centering, quiet. Above

the aviary's bluridescence:
a never-not-visible, fine-meshed, permanent net.

Bad Lion

What makes lion abhor
lioness? Aware
of danger, she abandons
her pride to hide them, lure
the angry, agitating one
who acts not like a lion
but like a criminal, since even
lions to lions can wrongly
behave. This one is
"murderer," "destroyer," "rapist."
He tortures the lioness,
severs her spine.
She takes their pain,
her daughters', sons',
into herself, buying time,
a little more. For them
she lets him tear her,
leave her on the dirt
to suffer, fade—

why must there be
a body to absorb
the line of hate?

Experience

Dream Needle

I was a maze of scars, the one
I remember most a seam from my chin
to my throat down to my navel. Some

point dragged me open. Some
hands prevented all from being spilled.
And there was thread, gone now,

that no longer matters, but whose memory
matters. A needle in a hand
stitched marks precise as calligraphy

which bound, then fell away.
When others saw the scars
they questioned and I wept, wanting

to hide, but needing recognition.
Back in my ordinary skin, I listen
for how chambers in a cage can move.

Behind such walls we resound. As bones
even, we are responded to.

Unfinished

and carved until I set him free . . .
—attributed to Michelangelo

I can try to explain how my body
passed around was inconsequential
to me, so much meaningless skin,
as if something behind it I was
digging, digging to find, dissolving
the idea of flesh, was a part of that—
or was it somebody's idea on my tongue?

The Flesh, it may as well have been, as much
as I understood it. Canopy
over a fire. A strained and billowing
fabric. Even if
the growing of perceptible desire
moved in me, it was so shapeless

it wouldn't be that they could help me find it
but that they were a place of my unbinding,
even their carelessness, their fumbling
moans. They never touched me
in spite of all that grappled slick
because I was asleep inside. Sex
was the stone.

Fourteen

Some days to be inside herself is hell,
walking down some street or hall,
wishing she were invisible
to all of them, but still in the middle, held.

Not wanting them to tear into her world
she inhabits a paradox: the world
should prop her with its things and people
who don't know how she feels

unless she lets it spill. (She will
not let it spill.) Her unpracticed voice
grows fainter. Her eyes contract to minimal
black cones dragging in the light

and heat of others, tiny
engines for imagining.

Fifteen

No reason for her to walk in moonlight
but she somehow believes there is. The same day
glared past. The same high sun on asphalt.
The same wilted leaves. The same confused brood
of inclinations. Things are too defined,
the hours rimmed like lakes on a map.
But in moonlight, she can enter a landscape
full of vagueness, a body of air
violet and permeable. She shivers
to feel it: her life is about to enter.
Someone's about to touch her arm,
his different voice making her turn
from this driveway to stride into other nights
beyond these, beyond any room of her grandmother's.

The Visit

She let him in the house. She let him in,
her mother still at work, the afternoon
stale with constant solitude and boredom.

She let him in the door and let him do
to her just what he wanted: press her down
on the flimsy unmade bed, and then press in

while she, not knowing how to make it good
for her, lay there and moved a little too.
He'd walked to this unfamiliar part of town

for a girl who barely talked but asked him in
to see and touch her (as she would again
if she sensed he had the inclination to),

so he was glad, after that stretch, to be rapt
in his own act. If she could make him
pleasure her instead of gray and sad

after-the-fact, the soiled air of her bedroom
when he left might not be so devoid of sun.
But that was her youth: big things vaguely done.

Exhilarated, Walking Past High Trees . . .

Exhilarated, walking past high trees,
I felt myself alone as always,

felt familiar daylight sear
it shut, that separation like a tear

behind me as I left the house. No pause
when we were done: he'd closed the door

on a place inside his heart and in his bed
(*what I deserved, a man was giving me*),

mute. Respectful, I had followed.
As if I were a jewel, for a while he'd led

with a fixed attention no one ever had
then talked until I felt him watching me,

hidden. We'd shared the drink, a joint,
had soaked the clump of fabric,

my eyes into the pillow. So,
"It's not supposed to hurt like this"? I turned.

Experience

—1979

"It's not supposed to hurt like this." I turned
my eyes into the pillow so
they soaked the clump of fabric and were
hidden. We'd shared the drink, a joint,
then talked until I felt him watching me
with a fixed attention no one ever had
as if I were a jewel. In a while, he'd led
me to his unlit bedroom. I had followed
mute, respectful, sensing that, at last
someone was giving me what I deserved,
a place inside his heart and in his bed.
When we were done, he closed the door
behind me as I left the house, no pause.
It hurt—that separation—like a tear.
But soon I felt familiar daylight sear
my pupils, felt myself alone as always,
exhilarated, walking past high trees.

"Laying Out"

A way to pause our bodies—
the heat paralyzing, radio buzzing, *Hit Parade*

and a dog-eared Danielle Steele beside me
on my hot towel on the concrete balcony

of my grandmother's apartment or behind
my best friend's condo, weeping glasses

of oversweetened tea her mother mixed us,
ice cubes diluting fast. On Saturdays,

Casey Kasem's American Top 40
gripped us, words we joked in between,

rotating, glistening, squinting
as the song names counted down,

our bodies prostrate and our minds
blank, or nearly blank. I loved it.

Being nothing but what we were. Light
not stroking us to unfold

bundled in our nylon swimsuits
but letting us be, soaked in a present

empty of peril, and amorphous.
What did we dream of, without poetry?

Hardly imagined. Near sleep.

Want Poem

In time, we won't get what we want
but also we won't want, since want
leaves us with our bodies—

the larger want, the smaller wants,
such immaterial differences won't
matter, just as matter won't

(though I know things shouldn't matter now
or later). But I am my want
sometimes—am an enormous want

and even when I'm not, can sense
it in the background, mountainous
hollow, breathing. It finds me out.

Mirror Mirror

A body is a body
not a shelf
on which to stack a thing
for someone else.

A palm's a palm.
A thigh's a thigh,
all imperfections less
outward than eyed

from within. The skin
bending, and bone,
cells—these frame
movements to own,

establish. So arch,
acknowledging
each (any) speck.
You feel to see.

Scissors

She used them on my hair
when I was a girl
snarled, unstill

and on the smile
of the boy, too old,
who rode a motorcycle

and on the lie I told
about the motorcycle
and on his call

(she could tell
if I was sly, or bad)
and on the will

that swelled
when I disobeyed,
the winter air that filled

the Catholic girls school,
the window sill
I climbed out of

wanting to feel
a boy's lips—snip! snip!
—on the parsley leaves

for her clam spaghetti,
on a strip of duct tape
for the loose screen door,

on the invisible
snake that crawled
into my room

after I took acid,
on a little truth
inside some answers.

She did not
use them on the years, or
on all my tears.

(How sever water?)
They were heavy, old,
black and silver.

She used them on my hair
and to cut
the thread she needled

to sew the coat
that fell apart
with me inside it

as I was once inside her.
For all of this, for more,
she held the scissors.

Adjusting to Darkness

1

For a while I've been considering nothing,
the nothing my grandmother refused
and my grandmother's grandmother,
all of them stretching back
through the void with their kinds of certainty
bracing the light of the stars.

2

In the Methodist church, my grandmother
opened her hymnal, her lips opening
with the surge of voices in the chamber,
the bodies of church members
lined up on either side of her like piano keys,
their mismatched pitches
staggered and chimed.

3

I like to think of her eyeing
brass candlesticks at the altar
and a minister's black and white cloth,
the minds around her
all thinking about the same thing
or trying to—a harmonious trying—

4

and to think of her reading the bible
in bed before she turned off
the lamp and turned to sleep,
her hair on a pale blue pillowcase,
her eyes upholding the tarnished
gold edges, the ivory horizon
behind words after they closed.

Spilled Milk on Banjo

when the dogwood petals begin to fall
a glass of milk knocked over on the grass
like the glass I spilled on my mother's banjo
a skin of change across the morning
table she'd laid it on when I was six
when the dogwood petals begin to drift
then I am less and when they are torn
in a startling hard spring rain I am
unmoored as the tree is ripped
so all its milky petals on the ground
just disappear they will not return
no more excursions from the branch
this year the banjo my mother stroked
with her clicking silver finger picks
like claws like a machine gears flashing
faster and faster her curved hands
raking across the strings such ringing
echoes from that hollow drum
and its tightened skin by accident
on the glassy disk of her instrument
I knocked the glass of milk so quickly it
ran I think I laughed then thinking
change was pretty overlaid silver skin
thin running liquid when the dogwood
leaves begin to fall—no, *petals*—leaves
still hang their secrecies tenacious
but without the incandescent spread
across the morning and at night
amid the other darknesses petals
flaring a skeletal miracle
I am sad girls are indelicate banjo
strings taut in their silver girdle
sharp in memory as my mother
calls out the petals already fallen
which tells us spring is over now forget

"Inspiration and Impediment"

—Adam Zagajewski

Twice now the hawk's mistake
landed her on the screened-in porch,

its mesh neatly invisible
to her arriving arc that tore.

Clear as a piece of furniture
she stood on a table, legs

taut, talons awkwardly steadying
on that odd level surface,

her crescent head, her shoulders'
pyramids, her hooded looking

around in quick, bladed turns
of the neck a sort of sovereignty

splintered into beatings
flung from her clutched and winging

at the screen. We got her out
for a second time, unbroken.

Ushered her, frantic, blind
to the opened door

until she swung up
and rare. We'll fix the screen

again. But the fact is, the fact airs
her in.

A Moth

—Elizabeth Bishop, 1931

She passed the asylum on each train ride,
the separate but linked cars
gliding along the rails,
getting close then moving on
again. She came, she went,
unlike her mother, sent
years before. Whether she watched
it rise in sight, whether she looked
or didn't, whether remembered or
forgotten, she passed the asylum, head in
a book or eyes on people, hills
and lakes, ignoring it, stern and leaden,
hardened to what it was. *Forget,*
remember, intrepid passenger,
the scorned the loved details.

Stemming from Stevens

It's not enough to cover the rock with leaves
—as if vernal fluidities

could be enough for the stern assault of fact.
As if a living ornament,

light and subject to temporal breezes,
could be enough to overcome despair,

that chunk of something solid in the air,
unmoving, as words repeated are.

It's not enough to cover despair
with motion. Motion itself is flawed,

continuous motion a narrow, thin escape
from what is rooted. Leaves do sway,

but in truth, they're only flapping out,
ancillary, uncertain, buffeted

this way and that. They remain the fact
they are bound to, involuntary notions

victim to the weather of a day,
gripped by what has thrust between the rocks,

flexible as everything not rock is,
reckless as imagining is reckless.

Suite for Bonnefoy

"As though the faraway
were already begun here."

1

You Let Them Live Inside You, More Transparent . . .

Than if they did not live, did not grow,
since solid stuff is often dead stuff,
immovable, detaching. You

let in their prying clearness
as a field allows a field
to become, not toward less chaos

but toward the ragged ends
of incompletion, more
transparent because you've leaned

toward kinds of them before,
have memorized their stalking
contours, holes,

and falters, bends. And gave
them room to dig in at all.

2

"Becoming Again a Threshold"

Whether illusion or truth
before illusion, or truth behind,

there is a door. There must be.
A door inside usual. In you

as you think of it, when you travel,
mapping your mind. Go,

become again a threshold.
You can cross over.

Though it is like nakedness
in an empty room, to linger

without choosing one, to linger
because you have to choose.

Waver inside
that rapid *begin.*

3

Those Rooms Inside, Too Far for Me to Enter

Those rooms inside, too far for me to enter
and the forms of objects trapped there, shadows
of things, the real things held inside some past,

the shadows memory's buildings—what else
do you find there, walking in mind, as if you
walked through spaces, cluttered, you can't reach

for? I want to *think* you lifting
one thing you now see, or lowering it
so you can, under memory's outlines

that stain hands, allow this blink
of light.

4

"He Dwells in the Tree of That Book. . ."

His long fingers sweeping
dry elements. Dwells
without food or drink, in stale air
as he corridors those passageways
wry as they are. The book's
tree doesn't need to be watered
except by his blood, the small
moisture of his quiet breathing.
Though the trunk was already there
and the stumping last branches,
their phantom array like a fan,
it elongates strange fronds as he watches.
When he sleeps, they draw back in the ground.

5

To an Interior

You are you. But in the while
you've changed yourself, meeting

that ghost of you who wanted to slip down
because it was faster,

reducing you partway, the others
crowding around the door,

impressing, cooing.
You must not allow

this next. For next will be an hour
you've never stitched. Consider

the perversions of metaphor—
what is true

rhymes less with what was named
if you surprise yourself. It doesn't matter.

To be surprised is to inhabit,
to have inhabited

so deeply you are wandered
till a hand, on your shoulder, stops.

Sheer Columns

How do we know it's not matter that matters
but matter's absence, elegies of matter

like air between the columns of these trees:
not lines of wood but lines of air between

the trunks' sticks, the thin spaces that aren't wood,
clear stalks grown up beside the solid lines,

those breezy hollows filled with non-existence?
I've seen what happens to a body's absence:

grief fills up an arid space that grows
bleak, empty spaces reaching for the light

then fading to a watery, sheer background
like space between these trees night's flimsy

winds tilt slightly. —Lines of air.
Maybe real trees shouldn't matter

more than surrounding stalks of air.
Let's see both trees and space for what they are:

a grove of roseate fading, dusky columns
showing us how wooden trunks defer

to lines of gray-pink, dimmed, dividing light
clear emptiness curves over. Who's to say

the mingled light and shadow stalks that grow
between trees as trees waver out of view

at dusk, aren't the best evidence of trees?
If things are always outlined by the space

around them, isn't absence what they are?
Shouldn't we treasure sheer columns more?

World's Witness

To continue to imagine between the cracks,
grappling inside a crevice, like

a chit, sprout, shoot, or semaphore. To
continue to imagine: milked abyss,

old bleak place filling up with fire, with spangles: that's
too involving opposites: dark/light,

moon stuck on a velvet backdrop, starched
and brooded, theatrical. To con

oneself into imagining that between
things' long-established contours there is room

to begin, intrude, continue to intrude, in spite
of abstractions and concrete, rooting

for the mind before world's whiteness folds
it in—or my own weakness.

Virtuosity

Tintoretto recreates the heroic idiom . . .
in terms of his own slashing virtuosity.
—Robert Echols

The cutting into what is there.
The cutting away. Or rather, the cutting out
of shapes and figures so they jut in air.
The jutting, cutting violence of some art.

Bravura, they call it. *Virtuosity.*
It shows what an artist did so we can see
not just creation but the artist's vigor
in it: the skillful tugging into space

those skins and limits of an object's substance
in culminations nature didn't build
(though some will say it's all nature's expanse
in the end, since art's invention spills

beyond what things have been, as a tendril
arcs toward sun). Minds can be changed
by an artist's hand, which clears
a viewer's first conception of a thing

(a tree, angel, or person) out of the way—
you might say "rips" or "tears" as art makes way,
slashing apart the established air
around us, like the removal of a veil

from a face. Old stories take new shapes:
twisted, reaching, emanating light—
We feel ourselves turn hopefully but vaguely.
We grope and fail and try and try and try.

Out of Doors

for Mark Strand

What is it we're waiting for,
the book held in our hands, staring at words
or furniture or memory?

The dark has nothing to do with us
beside the burning lamp, in the room
of vigilant forgetting

but there is someone out there
walking, always walking, away from here
not because of who we are

but because there is no chance for him to move
toward more of himself other than
through that darkness, one particular way.

Name

I'm not the one you fell for.
She died a few years before,
her name a world in a word
that holds more than I hear.

Like a globe with its painted world,
our life, the one you turn toward,
believing its vacant colors
and lines, since they've occurred

to us. But they're not yours.
Because you knew another.
I believe we give ourselves over
to one life. You found yours

for a little while. Though it's clear
you never *owned*.—No owner
despite trust. After the terror
of loss, you form the word.

Tourism

As the hawk carries the living creature
by the skin of its nape, through clear skies
across the interstate so low we can see it,
optimism is gripped and paralyzed

though the ocean was lovely today, its retractions
flaying the sand a kind of noise
I like, the shells abraded
gnarled trinkets that still please the eyes,

and the two of us rising and rising
as we try to do, in the ways we can,
like returning to a small clean tourists' cottage
in a town that is not our town.

After the hawk carried the living creature
in the air above us to the other side
of the interstate, for minutes I could not
not think about it still being awake

experiencing. But the thing is done.
Its bones are bone. And I am some
scene of disenchantment, out of reasons
for clinging to my optimism, gone

(the thing hunched helpless, carried higher
than it had known, in an attenuating sweep)
as the hawk carries the living creature
through clear skies, by the skin of its nape.

Advance

In the small light of morning,
everything comes clear.

Autumn dogwood's red berries,
starred with black stems, convex light,

their motionless leaves lilac-rimmed.
Maples turned overnight. Yellow

fumes from green, orange from yellow,
colors proved certain by contrast,

by change.
When you walk into that light

hang your sleep on a chair.
Hang your lethargy.

Wind nudges a thin, glistening layer
of dew over fronds. Air

seethes with the odor
of rinsed cones, of pines immured

in damp silence.
Stay, new conception. Endure.

I can see you, legs taking up chunks
of the landscape, abandoning

the place you imagined
you stood only moments ago.

Wing

People can remove themselves from us.
I don't mean death. I mean another
undeniable turning, like a wing
we never noticed suddenly swinging
open, visible in ways only we see:
Oh—she has the power to move that way.
As once-included ones, we face
the mute, familiar angles of a face,
its histories we thought transparent,
its banks of flesh. A different glance
charged with some fresh need or ancient
ugly failure re-arisen
for reasons we should know, and sometimes
do, and sometimes never do.
Affection is grace after all
and we are at its mercy.

Sea Heart

(*entada gigas*)

Laced through leaf canopy
long woven, like the bean stalk
of legend, voluminous vine,
a harboring trellis
of linked pods, you (a seed)
are hollow, heart-shaped, grained
dark as mahogany
and resistant to ruin, until rain
washes you out of the forest
toward river, then sea
for the tolerant glide
inside waves in which, nicked
by fish, turtles, wind, you'll sail
nowhere on purpose, will
be pummeled, and punctuate
battering currents
like a dash in one tedious sentence,
bobbing up through tides
until beached, maybe
Norway, maybe Florida, exotic
surprise. You can float
for years. You have that buoyancy.
They call you *fava de Colon,*
"Columbus' bean," and say
it was you that, strewn
on Portugal's shore, a landed echo,
led him to think there was more.

Glass Chimney

for Rachel Wetszteon

Since the bees have settled there for summer
I imagine it made of glass,
its corridor a throat with no language
but exquisite small gestures of bees
and imagine their vowelled hums
a proverbial chorus of murmurers
like the packed Sistine Chapel after ushers
have told us to *Sshhhh!* for a third time—
first silence, then a steadily growing wave
of our willfulness rising and rising,
chit-chat hymnal, contrapuntal—*Sshhhh.*

Bees chose this house, this chimney.
They crawl up and down its bricks
with a hurried vocation, nuns to their habits
and ritual drones. There are hundreds
of cells to the hive which, if under glass,
would shimmer like verses in "honeyed light."

But the bees' will in motion! The "will of the hive"
and the Queen being tended, abdomen stroked!
Not beauty, but engorgement, encouragement,
which is as it should be at the center of the hive!
No stings, and praise around that immoral center
which hotly expands and breeds. Keep the brood cells clean
and tender. Let the Queen fatten
so no violence supplants her. And may the hive swell
as frost cracks petals of imagined glass flowers.

Notes

Opening epigraph: Charles Bergman, "Hunger Makes the Wolf" (Chapter 1), *Wild Echoes: Encounters with the Most Endangered Animals in North America.* Urbana and Chicago: University of Illinois Press, 2003.

"Mayhem": I observed "Mayhem" (a giant octopus) at the Seattle Aquarium in January 2012. She died a few months later, having been released into the bay to give birth.

"The Swallow that Hibernates Underwater" is the name of a chapter in Daniel Quammen's book *Wild Thoughts from Wild Places.*

"Transparent Journey" is inspired by some details in the story "The Glass Mountain," contained in *The Yellow Fairy Book,* edited by Andrew Lang.

The opening line of "A Moth" is inspired by the following quotation: "Bishop never saw her again, even though as a young woman she passed the asylum on each train ride to Vassar College." (Rodney Phillips, *The Hand of the Poet: Poems and Papers in Manuscript.* New York: Rizzoli International Publications, 1997. Page 221.)

"Inspiration and Impediment": this phrase comes from (and the poem is inspired by) an essay written by Adam Zagajewski and published in *The Threepenny Review* (Issue 128, Winter 2012).

"Suite for Bonnefoy": the title "Becoming Again a Threshold" is taken from a phrase spoken in an interview with Yves Bonnefoy conducted and translated by John Naughton. The title of "He Dwells in the Tree of that Book" is also from a phrase in the interview (taken entirely out of context). The interview is contained at the end of the collection *In the Shadow's Light* (Yves Bonnefoy, translated by John Naughton).

Acknowledgments

I am grateful to the editors of the following journals, in which these poems appeared, sometimes in an earlier form:

Alabama Literary Review: "Figural"

American Arts Quarterly: "Virtuosity"

Blackbird: "Aquatic Herd," "Brooding Eels," "To an Exterminator"

Cincinnati Review: "Name," "Wing," "Blind Crevasse"

Crab Orchard Review: "Fifteen"

The Dark Horse (Scotland): "The Visit"

The Emily Dickinson Bulletin: "Mayhem"

Image: "Adjusting to Darkness"

Literary Imagination: "Thelonious"

The Louisville Review: "Scissors," "Villa Medusa"

Measure: *A Journal of Formal Verse:* "A Moth"

Memorious: "Gazelle in the House," "Becoming Again a Threshold," "Sea Heart"

The Missouri Review: "Octopus," "Oceans," "Anemone"

The New Republic: "Leaving the Field"

Orion: "Advance"

Poetry: "Stemming from Stevens," "Torch"

Poetry Daily: "Stemming from Stevens"

Poetry Northwest: "Fiddler Crab"

Raritan: "Bells Buried under the Sea," "Sounding Line"

Shenandoah: "Spilled Milk on Banjo"

Southwest Review: "Sheer Columns," "Desert Appearance"

Think Journal: "Experience"

Your Impossible Voice: "Nucleolus," "Mistral"

Sugar Mule: "The Glass Chimney"

Verse Daily: "Wing"

I am grateful to the Kentucky Arts Council for a 2010 Al Smith Individual Artist Grant, which helped support the writing of these poems, to the Museum of Fine Arts Houston and the Dora Maar Foundation for a Brown Foundation Fellowship to France where some of these poems were written, to my students and colleagues at Centre College for their thoughtfulness, curiosity, and support, and to my family.

photo by Chandler Williams

Lisa Williams was born in Nashville, Tennessee and has lived in Kentucky since 2001. She has been awarded the Rome Prize in Literature, the Barnard Women Poets Prize, and the May Swenson Poetry Award, and her poems have been featured in *Best American Poetry 2009*, *Bright Wings: An Illustrated Anthology of Poems About Birds*, *Best American Erotic Poems: 1800-Present*, and on *Poetry* and *Verse Daily*. She teaches at Centre College.

The Green Rose Prize

2013: Ralph Angel
Your Moon

2012: Jaswinder Bolina
Phantom Camera

2011: Corey Marks
The Radio Tree

2010: Seth Abramson
Northerners

2009: Malinda Markham
Having Cut the Sparrow's Heart

2008: Patty Seyburn
Hilarity

2007: Jon Pineda
The Translator's Diary

2006: Noah Eli Gordon
A Fiddle Pulled from the Throat of a Sparrow

2005: Joan Houlihan
The Mending Worm

2004: Hugh Seidman
Somebody Stand Up and Sing

2003: Christine Hume
Alaskaphrenia
Gretchen Mattox
Buddha Box

2002: Christopher Bursk
Ovid at Fifteen